W9-CIQ-602

# Wayne Gretzky

## Additional Titles in the Sports Reports Series

**Andre Agassi**
Star Tennis Player
(0-89490-798-0)

**Hakeem Olajuwon**
Star Center
(0-89490-803-0)

**Troy Aikman**
Star Quarterback
(0-89490-927-4)

**Shaquille O'Neal**
Star Center
(0-89490-656-9)

**Charles Barkley**
Star Forward
(0-89490-655-0)

**Jerry Rice**
Star Wide Receiver
(0-89490-928-2)

**Ken Griffey, Jr.**
Star Outfielder
(0-89490-802-2)

**Cal Ripken Jr.**
Star Shortstop
(0-89490-485-X)

**Wayne Gretzky**
Star Center
(0-89490-930-4)

**David Robinson**
Star Center
(0-89490-483-3)

**Michael Jordan**
Star Guard
(0-89490-482-5)

**Barry Sanders**
Star Running Back
(0-89490-484-1)

**Jim Kelly**
Star Quarterback
(0-89490-446-9)

**Deion Sanders**
Star Athlete
(0-89490-652-6)

**Shawn Kemp**
Star Forward
(0-89490-929-0)

**Junior Seau**
Star Linebacker
(0-89490-800-6)

**Mario Lemieux**
Star Center
(0-89490-932-0)

**Emmitt Smith**
Star Running Back
(0-89490-653-4)

**Karl Malone**
Star Forward
(0-89490-931-2)

**Frank Thomas**
Star First Baseman
(0-89490-659-3)

**Dan Marino**
Star Quarterback
(0-89490-933-9)

**Thurman Thomas**
Star Running Back
(0-89490-445-0)

**Mark Messier**
Star Center
(0-89490-801-4)

**Chris Webber**
Star Forward
(0-89490-799-9)

**Chris Mullin**
Star Forward
(0-89490-486-8)

**Steve Young**
Star Quarterback
(0-89490-654-2)

# Wayne Gretzky

## Star Center

Frank Fortunato

**Enslow Publishers, Inc.**

44 Fadem Road        PO Box 38
Box 699             Aldershot
Springfield, NJ 07081   Hants GU12 6BP
USA                       UK

**Library of Congress Cataloging-in-Publication Data**

Fortunato, Frank.
    Wayne Gretzky, star center / Frank Fortunato.
        p.  cm. — (Sports reports)
    Includes bibliographical references (p.  ) and index.
    Summary: Profiles the personal life and professional career of the
star center for the New York Rangers who has earned the reputation
of being the greatest hockey player ever.
    ISBN 0-89490-930-4
    1. Gretzky, Wayne, 1961–  —Juvenile literature. 2. Hockey players—
Canada—Biography—Juvenile literature. [1. Gretzky, Wayne, 1961–  .
2. Hockey players.] I. Title. II. Series.
GV848.5.G73F67   1998
796.962'092—dc21
    [B]                                                        97-20163
                                                                  CIP
                                                                  AC

Printed in the United States of America

10 9 8 7 6 5 4 3 2

**Photo Credits:** Doug MacLellan/Hockey Hall of Fame, pp. 10, 68, 81, 90;
Graphic Artists/Hockey Hall of Fame, p. 28; Hockey Hall of Fame, pp. 17,
33, 74; Miles Nadal/Hockey Hall of Fame, pp. 45, 58, 65, 94; Ottawa
Citizen/Hockey Hall of Fame, p. 22.

**Cover Photo:** AP/Wide World Photos.

# Contents

**1** The Great One . . . . . . . . . . . . . . . . . 7

**2** The Boy from Brantford . . . . . . . . 13

**3** The Rookie Sensation . . . . . . . . . . 27

**4** Dynasty! . . . . . . . . . . . . . . . . . . . 43

**5** Dark Clouds of Adversity . . . . . . . . 55

**6** King of the Kings . . . . . . . . . . . . . 61

**7** Injury and Comeback . . . . . . . . . . 73

**8** The Greatest One . . . . . . . . . . . . . 85

Chapter Notes . . . . . . . . . . . . . . 97

Career Statistics . . . . . . . . . . . . . 101

Where to Write . . . . . . . . . . . . . . 102

Index . . . . . . . . . . . . . . . . . . . . . 103

# Chapter 1

# The Great One

On March 23, 1994, the Los Angeles Kings were facing an uphill battle to gain the last spot in the National Hockey League's (NHL) Western Conference playoffs. Even though the team was struggling, a sellout crowd of some sixteen thousand people packed the Great Western Forum in Los Angeles to watch the Kings play the Vancouver Canucks. The applause in the arena was loud and long when "The Great One," Wayne Gretzky, took to the ice. The sellout crowd was also there in hopes of seeing Gretzky break one of hockey's most important and glamorous records—all-time career goals.[1]

When Gretzky, who already held sixty-two NHL records, scored career goal 801 on March 20, he tied

Gordie Howe for the all-time scoring record. It had taken Howe 1,767 games to score his 801 goals; Gretzky tied Howe's record in just 1,116 games. On October 15, 1989, Gretzky had broken Howe's record for career points (the total of goals and assists) when he scored a goal against his old team, Edmonton, for point 1,851. The all-time goal-scoring record, however, was proving to be somewhat more difficult for Gretzky.

Gretzky was going through a scoring drought. He had scored just three goals in the prior three weeks, partly because he had come down with the flu, which affected his play. There was another factor, however, to the record chase. Ever since Wayne Gretzky was a little boy, Gordie Howe had been his idol. Gretzky was challenging a mark set by his supreme hero. Though they were the two greatest scorers in NHL history, Howe and Gretzky were hardly carbon copies of each other, however. Gordie Howe was a big, tough player who was quite aggressive on the ice. Gretzky, at six-foot one-inch and 170 pounds, was small by hockey standards, and his gentle style of play was unusual in the violent world of professional hockey. Still, Howe and Gretzky both possessed a great drive to win *and* great admiration for each other. Howe, never one to mince words, told a reporter, "I am very respectful of Wayne. The record is falling into the hands of a decent man." He added, "Now if it was some jerk that might be different. I would be upset about that. But I like Wayne. I like his old man. I like the whole family."[2]

Through the first period of the game, Gretzky's stick remained silent. Then, at 14 minutes and 47 seconds into the second period, lightning struck. Vancouver defensemen Jiri Siegr drew a penalty for holding, giving Los Angeles a one-man advantage for the power play. The Kings' Luc Robitaille brought the puck into the Vancouver zone, passing to Gretzky, who was streaking on his left, towards the Canucks' net. Gretzky immediately fed the puck to his old buddy and teammate, Marty McSorley, who was racing down the right side. Vancouver goalie Kirk McLean came out of the net to cut off McSorley's angle, but McSorley skillfully sent the puck back across the crease to Gretzky, who took a quick wrist shot while the puck was still in the air. The puck rocketed into the empty net. It was done. The Great One had his sixtieth and greatest NHL record. As the Forum exploded into applause and cheers, Gretzky's teammates rushed onto the ice. The game was stopped for a videotape of highlights from the careers of Gretzky and Howe, and a ceremony was conducted at center ice. The first thing

*Wayne Gretzky loosens up before a game. As a member of the Los Angeles Kings, Gretzky shattered some of hockey's most prestigious records.*

Gretzky did when he got to the microphone was to thank the Vancouver Canucks for allowing the game to be interrupted for the ceremony. The final thing he said was, "Most importantly, life is nothing without family. I'd like to thank my mother and father and my wife, Janet. Thank you very much."[3]

That night, in Edmonton, Canada, where Gretzky had begun his NHL career and starred for ten seasons, the Oilers were hosting the New York Rangers. When Gretzky's record was announced over the public address system at Edmonton Coliseum, Oiler fans stood and gave The Great One a long ovation. Meanwhile, the Rangers' Adam Graves was setting a modest record of his own. During the Edmonton game, Graves scored two goals, giving him 51 for the season and making him the Rangers' all-time leading scorer. After the game, Graves was asked what he felt when Gretzky scored goal 802. "If I didn't have gloves on I would have been clapping too," Graves said. Then he added his personal thoughts about Gretzky: "I don't know him but I admire him. He's the biggest reason why hockey has expanded the way it has."[4]

**FACT**

On March 23, 1994, Wayne Gretzky scored NHL goal 802 against the Vancouver Canucks, making him the NHL's all-time goal-scoring leader.

# Chapter 2

# The Boy from Brantford

On display at Wayne Gretzky's restaurant in Toronto, Canada, is a tiny pair of ice skates. They were Gretzky's skates when he was two years old. Wayne Gretzky was born on January 26, 1961, to Walter and Phyllis Gretzky in Brantford, a Canadian town about sixty miles from Toronto. When Wayne was seven months old, his family moved from an apartment to a house in Brantford, but the family spent most weekends at Wayne's grandparents' farm outside of town. The twenty-five acre farm was Wayne's favorite place.

Wayne's father had been an amateur hockey player; in fact, all of the Gretzkys were avid hockey fans. On Saturday nights, on the farm, it was a family tradition to gather in front of the television to watch *Hockey Night in Canada*. During the program, two-year-old Wayne, using a small souvenir hockey stick and a foam rubber ball for a puck, practiced shooting goals between a pair of goal posts—grandmother Mary Gretzky's legs.

In November 1964, as soon as the Nith River was frozen over, Wayne's father whittled down a hockey stick and brought Wayne, who was wearing his first pair of skates, onto the ice. Walter Gretzky brought along his movie camera to capture his son's first steps (and falls) on the ice. Wayne had a great time, but it was cold, and soon they had to return to the farm house to warm up. That day, Wayne had his first case of chilblains (temporary swelling of the feet due to the cold). But he soon got over it and started coaxing his grandmother to sit in the big chair and play goal. On that day, Wayne Gretzky was two months shy of his third birthday.[1]

By the time he was four years old, Wayne was playing hockey every minute he could—at public rinks on weekends, but mostly on the river that ran through his grandparents' farm. However, Wayne's father had a problem with all the time Wayne was spending on the frozen river; his *own* feet were getting cold. So Walter Gretzky decided to build his son an ice rink in their backyard. He cut the grass, covered the frozen ground with half an inch of snow, and left the sprinkler on all night. The next morning, Wayne had his own practice rink. It was tough getting Wayne away from that backyard rink. Even his young friends would get tired and want to go home. When this happened, Wayne would use nickels to bribe his next door neighbor to keep playing.[2]

Meanwhile, the family's Saturday night ritual of watching *Hockey Night in Canada* on television was getting interesting. The family, particularly Wayne's grandmother, was faithful Toronto Maple Leaf fans. Mary Gretzky's favorite player was Frank Maholvich, but Wayne's supreme hero was Gordie Howe of the Detroit Red Wings. Wayne always rooted for Howe whenever Toronto played Detroit.

To this day, Gretzky maintains that his best Christmas memory was when he was five years old. He came downstairs on Christmas morning and found a Gordie Howe jersey under the tree. "I think I only opened up one other present," Gretzky says. "When I put that sweater on, it made my Christmas."[3] Wayne was small for his age, so small that his Gordie Howe jersey hung down to his knees, interfering with his shooting. Wayne started tucking the right side of his jersey into his pants, a practice he continues to this day, using Velcro™.

He wanted to play for a team, but minor-league hockey at the time started with ten-year-olds;

there was no room on the team for an undersized five-year-old boy. Walter Gretzky convinced his disappointed son that he needed to practice the fundamentals: "You look like you might have a size problem as far as hockey goes," he told Wayne, "but this can be overcome with puck control and concentration." So Wayne spent the next year in his backyard rink guiding the puck between pylons made of old plastic containers and anything else he could find, practicing puck control.[4]

Just before the start of the 1967–1968 season, a notice in the newspaper announced a tryout for the Brantford Atoms, a major novice team, (the first organized hockey team for children) in Toronto. At the tryout, tiny Wayne looked lost among the other boys, many of whom were ten years old. But the team's coach, Dick Martin, ignored Wayne's size and concentrated instead on his ability to skate. Wayne made the team. He scored just one goal during the season. At the time, no one could have possibly imagined where that goal would lead.

The following year, at age seven, Wayne scored 27 goals; at age eight, he scored 107; and at age nine, he scored an incredible 196 goals. Wayne was just warming up, however. At age ten, he scored 378 goals in sixty-nine games. Wayne was just four feet four inches tall. Strangers were now asking for his

*In 1967 Wayne Gretzky (#11) scored his first goal ever. Throughout his career, Gretzky's lack of size caused him to concentrate on his skating and stickhandling abilities.*

autograph, and he had caught the eye of the national media. This led to a meeting with his idol, Gordie Howe. "When you meet your heroes a lot of times you walk away saying, 'They aren't that nice,' or 'That was okay.'" Gretzky recalled, many years later, "When I met Gordie Howe he was bigger and better than I ever could have imagined."[5]

Meanwhile, Wayne's amazing scoring ability was infuriating some of the parents of the other kids. His teammates did not mind because along with the 378 goals, he had 120 assists—but their parents minded. Some took to timing Wayne with a stopwatch to see how long he held the puck. It got to the point where once, when Wayne was announced at the Brantford Arena, he was booed. The rest of Canada, however, was fascinated by this ten-year-old hockey player. John Herbert, writing in a London, Ontario, newspaper, called him "The Great Gretzky," a name that Wayne did not like at the time and still does not like, though it has stuck with him.[6]

When he was eleven years old, Wayne had a national article written about him. There were often times when he would play two games in two different cities on the same day. He was playing so much hockey that the jealous parents in Brantford were predicting that he would be washed up by the time he was twelve—burned out from too much ice time.

Wayne answered his critics by having a fifty-goal weekend. He scored fifty goals in nine games in a Hespeler, Ontario, Canada, tournament.[7]

Just before the first practice of his major pee-wee season at age twelve, Wayne desperately needed a new pair of gloves. Because of his small size, all of his equipment had to be light. The gloves also had to be flexible in order to help him feel the puck. Wayne and his father rushed into a store, but the only gloves that met these requirements were white. Walter Gretzky knew that Wayne would be labeled a "hot dog" if he wore white gloves. But, Wayne liked and needed the gloves, so Walter bought them. Sure enough, everywhere Wayne played he was taunted for wearing white gloves. By the end of the season, however, Wayne had scored 190 goals and often needed a police escort to get in and out of arenas due to the crush of fans. In Quebec City, the local team was drawing crowds of over eleven thousand people to see the kid in the fancy white gloves who they called "The White Tornado."

When Wayne was thirteen, he and his friend John Mowat decided to build the perfect hockey net in Wayne's cellar. They spent an entire Saturday building it. There was only one problem, the net was too big to fit through the cellar door; they had to cut the net into thirds to get it out. "I guess all the time

## FACT

The Stanley Cup is the oldest sports trophy competed for by professional athletes in North America. In 1893, Frederick Arthur Lord Stanley presented the Cup to the amateur hockey champions of Canada. The National Hockey Association took possession of the Cup in 1920. NHL teams have competed for the trophy since 1926, and it has been under the exclusive control of the NHL since 1946. When Lord Stanley originally presented the Cup in 1893, it stood 7 1/2" X 11 1/2" tall. The Cup now stands three feet tall, as additions were added to accommodate the names of every player on every Stanley Cup winning team. This trophy resides at the Hockey Hall of Fame in Toronto, Ontario, Canada.

on the ice froze our brains," Gretzky says when he tells the story. By age fourteen, as his national fame continued to grow, it had become difficult for Wayne to have a normal childhood in Brantford. His celebrity status was growing and a small minority of parents continued to pick on him at games, insisting that he would be burned out by the time he was fifteen. Also, Wayne and his parents knew that if he were to continue to grow as a hockey player, he would have to play against tough competition. That would mean moving to Toronto.[8]

Wayne's parents were concerned about him living away from home at such a young age. They worried that he might fall in with the wrong crowd in a big city like Toronto. But Wayne kept pleading, and deep down the Gretzkys trusted their son to stay out of trouble. Once they were certain that Wayne would be living with a nice family, they agreed. Now there was another problem. According to the junior hockey rules of that time, Wayne would have to play in the Metro Junior B Hockey league, a league with players as old as twenty years of age. Wayne was just fourteen years old and he weighed only 135 pounds. Some of the players were already married with families of their own. How would Wayne do against adult men?

Though he was the smallest and lightest player

in the league, and though he had to fight off a bout of mononucleosis (a flu-like illness that leaves its victims constantly drained of energy), he finished fourth in the league in scoring for his team, the Senecas, with 36 goals and 36 assists. He was voted Metro Junior B Rookie of the Year and his reputation kept growing. When he was fifteen, Canadian television ran a thirty-minute program entirely on Wayne. After two years of Junior B hockey, he was drafted into the Junior A League, one of the best amateur leagues in Canada.

Now there was another problem: Wayne was drafted by the Sault St. Marie Greyhounds, in a town some five hundred miles from Brantford. This time Wayne and his dad were in agreement, there was no way he was going to live five hundred miles from home. The Gretzkys conveyed their feelings to the Greyhounds' owner Angelo Bumbacco and Coach Muzz McPherson before the draft. The Greyhounds drafted him anyway, however, and after much coaxing, they convinced Wayne and his dad to take a plane ride to Sault St. Marie just to look around. Like a father-and-son chorus, the Gretzkys kept saying no as they drove around Sault St. Marie with Bumbacco who frantically tried to explain the benefits of playing there. Finally, in desperation, Bumbacco took the Gretzkys to the Budnars' house.

*Moving with the puck, Gretzky gets into position to make a big play. Gretzky was drafted into the Junior A League by the Sault St. Marie Greyhounds. Often, players will go directly from the Junior A League to professional hockey.*

Wayne had played junior hockey with the Budnars' son, Steve. When the Budnars said Wayne could live with them, Wayne instantly changed his mind. He would sign with the Greyhounds.[9] It was a decision that Wayne never regretted.

Since he started playing junior hockey, Wayne had always worn number 9, the number of his idol, Gordie Howe. Because 9 was taken on the Greyhounds, someone suggested number 99. This was a very high number for a hockey player, and it was feared that if Wayne wore it, he would be labeled a hot dog, but Wayne was used to that. More important to Wayne was the fact that NHL super-star Phil Esposito had recently been traded to the New York Rangers. His old number, 7, was taken, so he switched to 77. Esposito was the first NHL play-er to wear a high number. Wayne did not want Esposito to think that he intended any disrespect by copying his jump to a high number, so Wayne and his coach called Esposito in New York and asked him if he would mind if Wayne used 99. Esposito laughed and said, "Go ahead." Wayne has worn number 99 ever since.[10]

The transition from Junior B to A hockey went well for Wayne. In his first regular season game, he scored 6 points on 3 goals and 3 assists against the Ottawa 67's, and he just kept going. For the entire season, there was a three-way battle for the scoring title between Wayne, future NHL stars Bobby Smith of the Ottawa 67's, and Dino Ciccarelli of the London Knights. Bobby Smith took the title with 69 goals and 123 assists for 192 points, Wayne was second at 182 points (70 goals and 112 assists), and Ciccarelli was third with 144 points (72 goals and 72 assists). Wayne set new goal and assist records for a rookie, and was voted the league's most gentlemanly player with only fourteen penalty minutes. It was not a bad year at all—especially for a fifteen-year-old.

By the time he was seventeen, Wayne felt he was ready to make the jump to professional hockey, but the NHL had a rule preventing its teams from signing any player under twenty years of age. The NHL's rival league, the World Hockey Association (WHA), would do just about anything, however, in their fight for survival against the older, established NHL—including using orange pucks and signing seventeen-year-old amateurs like Wayne Gretzky. Gretzky attracted interest from several WHA franchises including Birmingham, Alabama, and Hartford, Connecticut. Wayne was interested in playing for Hartford because Gordie Howe, though now fifty-one years old, played for the Whalers. But the greatest interest came from Nelson Skalbania,

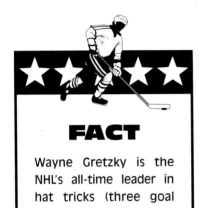

**FACT**

Wayne Gretzky is the NHL's all-time leader in hat tricks (three goal games).

owner of the WHA's Indianapolis Racers. Skalbania sent his private jet to pick up the Gretzkys and bring them to his home town of Vancouver, Canada, for an "interview."

"The way Nelson Skalbania interviews people is he runs with them until they're ready to drop," Gretzky recalled, years later, "I guess if you don't collapse in front of him, you're hired." Wayne and Skalbania ran seven miles together, and the last part was straight uphill. To impress Skalbania, Wayne sprinted up the hill, but Wayne could barely stand up. Later, he returned to his room where his father was waiting, "Oh, God, I'm dying!" Wayne said collapsing on his bed. "[Quiet], willya?" his dad whispered. "He'll think you're not in shape." The next day Wayne signed an $825,000 contract with Skalbania. The previous summer, Wayne had worked for five dollars an hour fixing potholes.[11]

Professional hockey never caught on in Indianapolis. Gretzky scored 3 goals and had 3 assists in eight games for the Racers, while attendance dwindled from a high of eleven thousand people to just over five thousand a game. Skalbania claimed he was loosing forty thousand dollars per game. A rumor began circulating that the WHA was about to fold and that the NHL would absorb the collapsing league's stronger teams. Because Wayne had signed a personal services contract with Skalbania, the Racers' owner had the right to sell Gretzky's services to the highest bidder. Both Winnipeg and Edmonton were interested.

Skalbania left the decision about where Gretzky would play up to Gretzky himself. After discussing it with family advisers, Wayne Gretzky and his dad chose Edmonton. They felt that Edmonton was the stronger team, more likely to be absorbed into the NHL. Skalbania honored his young star's request, selling Gretzky to Edmonton.

At the time, 1978, Edmonton, Alberta, was a rapidly growing area in Canada's Great Plains. Edmontonians, who mainly worked in the oil industry and on cattle ranches and farms, loved their new hockey team, the Oilers. Being Canadian, Gretzky knew something about cold weather, but, he had not known anything like what is experienced in Edmonton. Gretzky learned something of greater importance during his first meeting with Oilers coach Glen Sather, however: "One day we're going to be in the NHL and you're going to be captain of this hockey team. Remember I told you that."[12] Wayne gulped and nodded. He was still just seventeen years old.

# Chapter 3

# The Rookie Sensation

**D**uring his first week in Edmonton, Gretzky roomed with coach Glen Sather. He proved to his coach that his moves on goal were nothing compared to his moves on a refrigerator: "I've never seen a kid who eats like that one," Sather told reporters. "He eats more at meals than my whole family and he's always up for snacks."[1] But for all his eating, Gretzky barely weighed 160 pounds, making him a lightweight by hockey standards. Gretzky's next challenge was to prove he could stand up to a long, grueling professional hockey season.

Gretzky not only endured the rigorous schedule in Edmonton, but emerged as one of the best players in the league. Counting the eight games he played for Indianapolis, Gretzky played all eighty games of

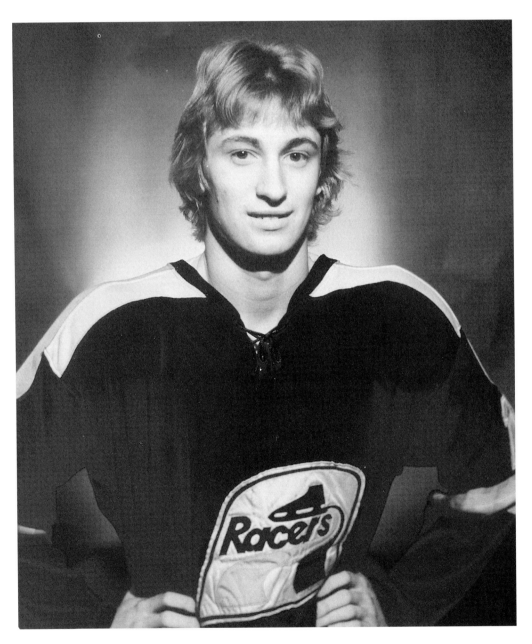

The first professional hockey team that Gretzky saw action with was the Indianapolis Racers of the World Hockey Association. The Racers went out of business and Gretzky was sold to the Edmonton Oilers, where he would finish his rookie year.

the WHA schedule. By mid-season his play was good enough to get him selected as a WHA second-team All-Star. This led to what was then the biggest thrill of his life: playing on the same line as Gordie Howe. The fifty-one-year-old Howe took the seventeen-year-old Gretzky under his wing. In the locker room prior to a game against a team of Russian All-Stars, Howe had Gretzky's jersey, which was interfering with his shooting, stitched to his pants. Then, in the opening seconds of the game, Howe set Gretzky up for a score. Later in the game, Howe helped Gretzky with a Russian player who kept hooking and chopping at Gretzky with his stick. Howe told Gretzky to flush off to his right when he saw the Russian coming, then stay out of the way. Howe delivered one of his devastating body checks.[2]

The WHA All-Stars swept the Russians in three straight games, the most thrilling games in Gretzky's young life. His play kept improving as the season progressed. By the end of the season, Gretzky's 46 goals and 64 assists were good enough for third in the league in scoring and Rookie-of-the-Year honors. Gretzky was now all of eighteen years old.

Following the 1978–1979 season, the news broke that the WHA was to be dissolved, with four of its teams, including Edmonton, being accepted into the NHL. Oilers' fans were ecstatic. Within eleven days of the announcement, all 15,242 seats in the Edmonton Coliseum were sold out for the coming season. Then, in the 1979 draft, the Oilers acquired two more promising young players in Mark Messier and Kevin Lowe. Messier, Lowe, and Gretzky would become and remain close friends as they rose to stardom together in the NHL.

Despite his outstanding rookie season, Gretzky was still hounded by critics. Players check hard in the NHL. The critics were saying that a small player like Gretzky would get bounced all over the ice. A writer for the Toronto Maple Leafs acknowledged that Gretzky had a fine rookie year in finishing third in scoring in the WHA, but said that there was no way he would finish third in the NHL. After Gretzky read the Toronto article, he publicly announced that he wanted to finish third in scoring in the NHL.[3]

Gretzky's first NHL goal came on October 14, 1979, at 18:51 in the third period against Glen Hanlon of the Vancouver Canucks. "It was a backhander," Gretzky recalls. "I came out of the corner and threw it over the top of Glen Hanlon. There's something special about the first goal you score in the NHL. You spend your whole life dreaming about it."[4] Fifty more goals followed over the course of the season, but it was a rocky road for Gretzky, who battled tonsillitis for the entire season. Coach Sather wanted him to have his tonsils removed, but Gretzky refused until the season was over. He did not want to miss a game. Despite the tonsillitis, Gretzky had 18 goals and 50 assists after fifty games; he was only twenty points behind Marcel Dionne and Guy Lafleur who were tied for the NHL scoring lead. Then, fully adjusted to the tougher and more demanding play in the NHL, Gretzky took off over the last thirty games of the season. He finished the season with 51 goals and 86 assists, tying him with Dionne for the league scoring title. Because Dionne accumulated one more goal than Gretzky, he was awarded the Art Ross Trophy as scoring leader. After Gretzky was awarded the Lady Byng Trophy as the NHL's most gentlemanly player, it was announced that he had also won the Hart Trophy, as the NHL's Most Valuable Player. By exceeding his publicly stated goal of finishing third in scoring, and by winning the MVP award, Gretzky finally silenced the skeptics. In the playoffs, the young Oilers were swept by the Philadelphia Flyers, but there was no longer any doubt that nineteen-year-old Wayne Gretzky was for real.

Gretzky's outstanding rookie season lead to a

**FACT**

On April 6, 1980, Wayne Gretzky won his first Hart Trophy as the NHL's Most Valuable Player. On the same day, Gordie Howe retired as a player. Gretzky has won more Hart Trophies than any other player in the history of the NHL.

new challenge—overcoming the sophomore jinx. The 1979–1980 season was the fifth straight season in which Gretzky had been a rookie in one league or another. Now that he had proven his ability among the best in the NHL, a new type of pressure emerged. Sure, he had performed like a pro in his rookie season in the NHL, but what would he do to follow it up? Would he fall victim to the notorious sophomore jinx that plagued so many athletes? This was a question for many—fans and critics alike—as the 1980–1981 season began.

Gretzky continued to amaze everyone during the 1980–1981 season. He finished with 55 goals and set new NHL records for assists (109) and points (164) in a single season. His performance won him his first All-Star team slot at center, his first Art Ross trophy as a scoring leader, and his second Hart trophy as league MVP. However, it was not just Gretzky, but the entire Edmonton team that was raising eyebrows, particularly after it swept the proud Montreal Canadiens in three straight games in the first round of the playoffs. Six of the Oilers—Wayne Gretzky, Mark Messier, Jari Kurri, Glenn Anderson, Kevin Lowe, and Paul Coffey—were still young enough to be playing junior hockey. Now, in the second round of the playoffs, this talented group of whiz kids had to

*Gretzky is shown here as a member of the Ontario Hockey League (OHL) All-Star team.*

face a dynasty team in the New York Islanders. The Oilers lost the series with the Islanders, but they played tough in most games. They did gain something invaluable in the defeat, however—experience. The Oilers' day would come—sooner then most people realized.

Because of expansion, better training methods, and a shifting style of play within the NHL, only one single-season record remained intact from pre-expansion days when the league had only six teams; Maurice Richard's fifty goals in fifty games, achieved during the 1944–1945 season. Even that record had been tied by the Islanders' Mike Bossy during the previous season. But now, thirty-nine games into the 1981–1982 season, Gretzky had a chance to break the record in fewer than fifty games. He had scored forty-six goals in the first thirty-nine contests of the season, ten in his last four games. In his last game against the Los Angeles Kings, he had scored 4 goals, but he had also hurt his knee, and it would not stop aching. On December 30, 1981, before the the next game against the Flyers in Edmonton, Coach Sather came into the locker room and handed Gretzky two aspirin. "Here," Sather said, "tape these to your knee." Gretzky laughed; he was so tickled by the joke that he did it. (He taped the aspirins beneath his kneepad before going out on the ice.) The aspirin might have done the trick. Gretzky reeled off two quick goals in the first period, another on a breakaway in the second period, and yet another after five minutes of the third period. The Oilers now led 4–1 and Gretzky had tied the record with 4 goals. Then the Flyers clawed their way back into the game, and they were trailing 6–5 with two minutes left on the clock. In a desperate effort to tie the game, Philadelphia pulled its goalie, Pete Peeters, out of the net in order to have another man up ice. Gretzky got the puck at mid-ice, aimed and fired at the empty net—but he missed. Then, with seven seconds left in the game, Glenn Anderson got a rebound and quickly fed Gretzky. With two seconds left, Gretzky fired off a shot—right into the net. His five-goal performance gave Gretzky fifty-one goals in thirty-nine games. The sellout crowd of 17,490 gave him a standing ovation that lasted long after the game had been completed.

With fifty-one goals under his belt in half a season, sportswriters now began predicting that Gretzky would break Phil Esposito's single-season scoring record of 76 goals. Gretzky was not so sure: "To hit 76 I'd have to get 26 goals in 40 games," he said. "Never mind what's happened so far, that's a lot of

**FACT**

On April 2, 1980, when he was nineteen years and two months old, Wayne Gretzky scored his fiftieth goal of the 1979–1980 season. This made him the youngest player ever to score 50 goals in a season.

goals." Some experts also felt Gretzky would score two hundred, shattering his own record of 164. It turned out that they were right, and it did not take Gretzky the full season to break both records. In the sixty-seventh game of the season, against Buffalo, Gretzky scored his seventy-seventh goal, setting a new record. By then, with five games remaining in the season, he has accumulated 199 points. Gretzky flew his parents into Calgary, the site of his next game, where they watched their son score point 200—an assist on a Pat Hughes goal, followed by two more goals. Usually, Gretzky received four thousand pieces of fan mail a week; while he was chasing Esposito's record, the letters increased to over ten thousand a week. Wayne Gretzky had electrified the world of hockey.

The slender center from Brantford was methodically rewriting the record books. Gretzky finished the season with phenomenal numbers; 92 goals, 120 assists, and 212 points—all new records, and by a wide margin.

The Oilers had finished the season with the second-best record in the NHL, after the Islanders. Their first-round opponents in the playoffs were the Los Angeles Kings, a team they had beaten by forty-nine points during the regular season. The Oilers' youthful enthusiasm made them feel invincible;

they headed into the playoffs in an overconfident frame of mind. Then the roof caved in. The Oilers lost to the Kings three games to two, losing the final game in Edmonton, 7–4. "They choked," said a headline in the *Edmonton Journal*. Another local paper called them, "weak-kneed wimps." It was a long summer for the Oilers, but they had learned an important if painful lesson—never take anything for granted.[5]

A more mature team took to the ice in 1982–1983. Now they did things as their coaches instructed, rather than playing the way they themselves thought they should play. Gretzky, picking up where he had left off the previous season, again led the league in goals (71), assists (125, bettering his own record), and points (196). Playing a more disciplined game, the Oilers made it all the way to the Stanley Cup Finals. There, however, they ran into a brick wall known as the New York Islanders. The Islanders were a dynasty powerhouse that had won the previous three Stanley Cups. They made it four straight by sweeping Edmonton in four games. The Oilers were a super-talented, exciting team that drew crowds wherever they played. On the road, they drew fourteen hundred more fans per game than the NHL average. But a dark cloud was gathering over the team—the reputation for not winning the big games. Soon that would change.

Prior to the 1983–1984 season, Oilers' veteran and captain Lee Fogolin named Wayne Gretzky team captain. Gretzky lived up to the honor. Beginning on opening night, he had a fifty-one-game point streak in which he scored an amazing 153 points on 61 goals and 92 assists. Gretzky finished the season with 87 goals and 118 assists, good for 205 points. The Oilers played to a record of 57 wins, 18 losses, and 5 ties. This was the first team in NHL history with three fifty-goal scorers—Gretzky, Glenn Anderson (54) and Jari Kurri (52). The Oilers breezed past Winnipeg in the first round of the playoffs, three games to none; then it took them seven games to get by Calgary before sweeping Minnesota in four straight. Now, once again, all that separated the Oilers from the Stanley Cup was the Islanders.

The schedule for the best-of-seven favored New York. The first two games would be played on the Islanders' home ice in Uniondale, Long Island. Then the series would move to Edmonton for three games before returning to New York for the final two contests, if necessary. The Oilers felt that it was critical to earn at least a split of the first two games in New York. In game one, Islanders' goalie Billy Smith was outstanding, holding the Oilers to just one goal. Oilers' goalie Grant Fuhr was better, however. He shut out New York for a 1–0 Edmonton win. In the second game, the Islanders bounced back, beating the Oilers 6–1. The series then moved to Edmonton for three games that the Oilers desperately wanted to win. They did not want to have to play the final two contests in New York.

Heading into the third game, Gretzky was leading the playoffs in total points including 9 goals. But none of these goals had been against the Islanders, who had shut him out so far. The Oilers took the third game, 7–2, but again, Gretzky had been shut out. The sportswriters zeroed in on Gretzky's drought: "Is Gretzky just a regular-season scorer who chokes during crucial games?" they asked. Gretzky took the criticism in stride. Edmonton led the series, 2–1. As long as they kept winning, Gretzky figured it did not matter *who* did the scoring. Finally, less than two minutes into the first period of game four, Gretzky took a perfect pass from Dave Semenko and skated down the middle, one-on-one against Billy Smith. Gretzky faked a shot to the left and Smith went for it. Then he fired to the right for a goal. In the third period, Gretzky stole the puck, streaked down ice, and beat Smith for another goal, this time unassisted. The Oilers won, 7–2. Just one victory now separated them from their first Stanley Cup.

Prior to game five, the Oilers were confident but nervous in their locker room. They felt they could nail down the Cup that evening, but if they lost, it would mean returning to New York, where the Islanders could still be lethal. As the game began, Gretzky took charge, converting two passes from Jari Kurri into two goals. With the Oilers leading, 2–0 at the beginning of the second period, the Islanders replaced goalie Billy Smith with Roland Melanson, but it did not help. Gretzky assisted on the third Oiler goal, and Kurri scored for a 4–0 Oiler lead by the end of the period. The Islanders stunned the crowd at Northlands Arena by scoring two goals in the first thirty-five seconds of the third period, then the Oilers tightened up their defense. With just thirteen seconds left in the game, Edmonton's Dave Lumley slapped a shot into the empty Islander net, sealing the game at 5–2. As the Oiler players hugged each other, a group of fans ran out onto the ice. One ran right up to Wayne Gretzky and jumped into his arms; it was his twelve-year-old brother, Brent. With the ice covered in balloons, the clock ran down to zero, and it was official: The Edmonton Oilers were the new Stanley Cup Champions.

Gretzky finished the playoffs as the scoring leader with 34 goals. Later, in the locker room, reporters asked Gretzky how he felt: "You know," he said, "there isn't a word I know that described this." One reporter wrote, "Someday Gretzky, Lowe, Coffey, and Messier will learn what to say. Perhaps after three or four more Cup victories."[6]

# Chapter 4

# Dynasty!

**G**retzky had been a hockey celebrity even since he was ten years old, but now that the Oilers were Stanley Cup Champions, the spotlight fell on him like never before. At just twenty-three years old, Gretzy was dominating the game of hockey like no other player had ever done before. People began to wonder what the secret to his success was. Surely it was not his size and strength. A five-foot eleven-inch, one-hundred-sixty-pound center was small in the world of hockey. And Gretzky was not exceptionally strong either. Gretzky's bench press of 140 pounds was the worst on the team, and during the Oilers' twice-yearly strength tests, he always finished last. Some experts guessed that Gretzky's nervous system "fired" faster than anyone else's, allowing him to react more quickly than other players. Most observers, however, credited his success to an instinctive ability to anticipate the path of the puck. Gretzky seems to know exactly where to skate in order to meet the puck. He credits hard work for most of his instinct. From as early as he can remember, his dad trained him to anticipate the path of the puck, and to skate to where it was *going*, not where it was.[1]

People marvel at Gretzky's ability to handle the puck. This he also credits to hard work. As a child, he practiced stick handling with a tennis ball. This was an exercise that trained him to pull pucks out of the air. Further, Gretzky feels his success is due, in part, to his ability to play behind the net. This is a maneuver he learned from Bobby Clark and refined into one of his trademarks. He feels that the net gives him a natural "pick" of protection. If a defenseman comes at him from one side, he can exit from the other side. If he is flanked from both sides, he can pass off to a teammate. In one game against St. Louis goalie Mike Liut, Gretzky was trapped behind the net by two defensemen on either side. So, he flipped the puck over the net, off Liut's back, where it bounced into the net for a goal.[2]

Despite their youth, their obvious talent, and the fact that they were the highest-scoring team in

*Trying to get open, Wayne Gretzky wards off a Toronto defender.*

hockey history, some people still insisted that the Oilers were not for real. Stan Fishler, writing for *Inside Sports*, predicted, "It's only a one-year dynasty for Gretzky and Team Arrogance."[3] Upon reading this, Gretzky set a secret goal of scoring two assists per game. But others were voicing skepticism as well, and Gretzky and his teammates began to wonder what it would take to win everyone's respect. They figured that winning another Stanley Cup would do the trick.

By the All-Star-Game break of the 1984–1985 season, Gretzky led the league with 54 goals; right behind him on his own line was Jari Kurri, with 52. In the Oilers' seventy-fifth game, Kurri scored his seventieth goal, breaking the all-time record for a right-winger. Kurri ended the season with 71 goals, two behind Gretzky's league-leading 73. Gretzky extended his own season assist record from 125 to 135; his 208 points were the second best in the history of the NHL (behind his own record of 212).

The Oilers clinched their division early; then following injuries to goalies Grant Fuhr and Andy Moog, they sputtered through the rest of their schedule, going 3–5–3 over the last eleven games of the season. Still, the Oilers finished the season with the second-best record in the NHL, with 109 points to Philadelphia's 113. In the first round of the playoffs, the Oilers swept past their usual postseason nemesis, Los Angeles, in three games—though they had to beat the Kings twice in overtime in order to do it. They then swept Winnipeg in four straight with Gretzky tying his own playoff record in game three by scoring seven points on a hat trick and four assists. Next came Chicago, where the fans where the loudest in the league, and the rink was fifteen feet shorter than Edmonton's. This tended to hinder the Oilers' free-skating style. The Black Hawks used Tom Murray to trail Gretzky at all times, a tactic Gretzky foiled by skating over to another Black Hawk and causing a four on three, leaving Kurri and Coffey open to score. Gretzky's tactic worked and Edmonton breezed past Chicago into the finals against Philadelphia.

It would not be easy to defend their Stanley Cup against the Flyers, who had beaten the Oilers in all three of their regular-season meetings. Their problems with the Flyers became quickly apparent as the Oilers lost the first game of the Stanley Cup finals, 4–1, in Philadelphia. Gretzky had a bad game, failing to get off a single shot on goal.[4] A *Philadelphia Inquirer* writer helped the Oilers cause by labeling Gretzky and Paul Coffey frauds for having an off game. Seeing red, Gretzky scored a goal in the first period of the second game, which along with a Will

Lindstrom goal, was enough to turn back the Flyers, 2–1. Philadelphia's problems with Gretzky were just beginning, however.

The series then moved to Edmonton for three games. In the first of these contests, Gretzky came out on the ice white hot, scoring two goals in the first seventy-five seconds. A third goal thirteen minutes later gave Gretzky a first-period hat trick. An assist later in the 4–3 Oilers' win gave him 41 points for the playoffs, breaking his own record of 38. The Flyers bounced back to take a 3–1 lead after the first period of game 4, but Edmonton tied the score 3–3, and went on to win, 5-3—on two Wayne Gretzky goals. The Oilers were leading the series 3–1. Another Oiler victory would give them their second Stanley Cup in two seasons; a loss would send the finals back to Philadelphia, a trip the Oilers did not want to take. Fortunately a Gretzky goal and three assists powered Edmonton over Philadelphia, 8–3. With Edmonton's successful defense of the Stanley Cup, the critics seemed to vaporize as if by magic.

Gretzky set new playoff records with an amazing 30 assists and 47 points. He also tied Mike Bossy and Jean Beliveau for most goals in a Stanley Cup Final, with 7. It seemed a toss up between Gretzky and Coffey as to who deserved the Smythe Trophy for MVP of the playoffs. The award was given to Gretzky.

With the Oilers back-to-back Stanley Cup winners, the spotlight fell on Gretzky as never before. He was now universally considered the best player in the world, and people wanted to know more than ever what made this hockey superman tick.

Gretzky considered 1985–1986 to be his best season. Though he only had 52 goals, the least since his rookie season, he had 163 assists, better than two a game. This achievement solidified his reputation as the greatest playmaker in the history of hockey. Gretzky's 163 assists and 215 points became personal records as well as NHL records, and they still stand to this day.

In sports, a team is considered a dynasty when it wins three consecutive championships. Before the 1985–1986 season began, most experts picked Edmonton to achieve dynasty status by winning its third-straight Stanley Cup. By the end of the regular season, it seemed that this prediction was right on target. The Oilers finished the season with a 57–17–7 record; their 119 points were best in the NHL, nine points ahead of runner-up Philadelphia. It looked like business as usual when Edmonton swept Vancouver in the first round of the playoffs by scores of 7–1, 5–1, and 5–1.

In the second round, Edmonton met Calgary, a team that had never defeated the Oilers in the playoffs.

## FACT

Wayne Gretzky is one of many professional athletes who is quite superstitious. In fact, superstitions are another department in which Gretzky regularly leads the NHL. He will not fly on Friday the thirteenth, nor will he get a haircut on the road. The last time he did, the Oilers lost. Before every game, he puts on his uniform in exactly the same way. On the ice, Gretzky always misses his first warm up shot; side right. Following the warm up, he always has a diet Coke™, followed by ice water, Gatorade™, and finally a second diet Coke™.[5]

But then an old ghost—overconfidence—returned to haunt the Oilers. Edmonton was stunned when Calgary won the first game of the series, 4–1. The Oilers bounced back to take the second game, 6–5, but Calgary played tough, and after six contests, the series was tied. The seventh and deciding game was played at Edmonton. As usual, Calgary played tough and after two periods the score stood tied at 2–2. Then in the third period, Steve Smith tried to clear the puck away across the crease from his own corner. Unfortunately the puck hit Oilers' goalie Grant Fuhr in the back of his left calf and skidded into the net. The freakish goal put Calgary up 3–2; the Oilers had thirteen minutes left to even the score, but they fell short. The Oilers' brilliant season came crashing to a halt two rounds short of the Stanley Cup finals. Wayne Gretzky won his seventh-consecutive Hart Trophy as the league's Most Valuable Player, but it was little consolation. The Oilers' dynasty quest had been put on hold.

The Great One added to his achievements during the 1986–1987 season. He again captured the scoring title with 62 goals and 121 assists, good for 183 points. Again, the Oilers had the best record in the NHL. But all of this was ancient history once the playoffs began. Mindful of their stinging early elimination in the previous season's playoffs, Gretzky and his teammates guarded against overconfidence as they headed into post-season play. They knew that regaining the Stanley Cup would be a tough task, but they did not realize just how difficult it would be. They quickly got an indication, as it took five games to defeat the Kings, four more to eliminate Winnipeg, and five more contests to get past Detroit. But the toughest part lay ahead.

Once again, the Oilers faced the Flyers in the finals. The two teams were opposites in style. The Oilers' success was based on great skating and an explosive offense. The Flyers' trademark was a powerful defense, anchored by sensational rookie goalie Ron Hextall.

The series began in Edmonton with the Oilers easily taking the first game, 4–2. But in the second game, Edmonton got a sense of what lay ahead in the series. With the score tied, 1–1, after the first period, Gretzky scored a goal on a power play just forty-five seconds into the second period. However, the Flyers fought back to tie the score at 2–2 at the end of regulation time, and the game went into overtime. In the second minute of overtime, Gretzky launched a rocket at the Flyers' net, completely freezing Hextall, but the shot hit the right post and bounced off the side. Then, four minutes later, with Hextall distracted by Coffey rushing up the slot,

## FACT

Wayne Gretzky has been a model of scoring consistency throughout his career. He holds the NHL record for most forty-goal seasons. He also holds the record for consecutive forty-goal seasons.

Kurri fired an angle shot from the left circle that sailed into the net for a 3–2 Oilers' win in overtime.

With the Oilers leading two games to none, the finals shifted to Philadelphia. In game three, breezing along with a 3–0 lead, the Oilers were jolted as the Flyers shut down the Edmonton offense and scored five unanswered goals for a 5–3 win. In game four, Gretzky put on a display of his skating and passing ability; his assist powered the 4–1 Edmonton win. With three games to one lead, and the series due to end in Edmonton, the Oilers seemed a sure bet to clinch their third Stanley Cup. Philadelphia, however, won the next two games, 4–3 and 3–2, tying the series at three games each. From a commanding 3 games to one lead, the Oilers found themselves in a sudden-death fight for survival.[6]

This was the first Stanley Cup Final to go to seven games in sixteen years. The deciding game was played in Edmonton. There was plenty of pressure on the Oilers as they took the ice. The pressure increased as the Flyers scored the first goal, but the Oilers responded with a goal by Messier off a perfect pass from Gretzky. Edmonton's defense then closed down Philadelphia as it methodically added two more goals for a 3–1 win and its third Stanley Cup. The crowd exploded.

For only the fourth time ever, a member of the

losing team, Ron Hextall, was voted the series MVP award. As team captain, Gretzky carried the Stanley Cup around the rink for the first victory lap. Then Gretzky handed the Cup to Smith in order to help the defenseman bury the pain of his mistake in the previous year's playoffs.

Back in the locker room, all of the Oilers agreed that this was the toughest series—and the sweetest. Edmonton had not won three-straight Stanley Cups, but they had accomplished the next best thing: winning three out of four. "We came back and showed who's best," Gretzky told reporters, "and it's still the greatest feeling in the world."[7]

# Chapter 5

# Dark Clouds of Adversity

**D**uring the 1987–1988 season, adversity came to Wayne Gretzky in the form of a pair of injuries. An eye injury kept him sidelined for two games, and a knee injury sustained in a game against Philadelphia kept him out of action for another sixteen games. A month after returning from the knee injury, Gretzky picked up assist number 1,050 in a game against Los Angeles, breaking Gordie Howe's all-time assist record of 1,049. Howe acquired 1,049 assists in 1,767 games. Gretzky notched his 1,050 assists in just 681 contests. The game was stopped, and Gretzky's closest friends on the Oilers, Mark Messier and Kevin Lowe, presented him with a gold hockey stick engraved with the names of all of the players he ever assisted. It is Gretzky's favorite hockey memento.[1]

The eighteen games Gretzky missed caused him to lose the scoring championship for the first time in nine years. He was unseated by Pittsburgh's Mario Lemieux, who with 70 goals and 98 assists accumulated 168 points, compared to Gretzky's 40 goals and 109 assists for 149 points. The Great One's absence also caused the Oilers to slip to third place in their division, but in one respect, Gretzky's enforced layoff proved to be a blessing. The time off left him rested and in mid-season form for the play-offs.

In the first round of the playoffs, Edmonton breezed by Winnipeg in three games. Many people, including Gretzky, felt that the Stanley Cup would be decided in the second round when Edmonton faced powerful Calgary—the leader in regular-season points. The Oilers took the first game of the series 3–1 with Gretzky contributing a breakaway goal. The second game was tougher. Trailing by two goals twice in the game, Edmonton was losing, 4–3, with several minutes left to play when Jari Kurri stole the puck from a Calgary defenseman and tied the score. A Messier penalty in overtime led to a dangerous Calgary power play. Then Gretzky let loose with a slap shot from the blue line. It sailed into the net over Calgary goalie Mike Vernon's shoulder, for a dramatic 5–4 win. Edmonton won the next two

**FACT**

Wayne Gretzky holds the NHL record for most one hundred point or better seasons.

games, 4–2 and 6–4, sweeping the series. The Oilers took Detroit in four games out of five. They headed into the Stanley Cup finals for the fourth time in five years.

The Oilers faced the Boston Bruins in the finals. The first three games of the series were played in Boston. The Oilers jumped to a quick two-game lead, taking the first two contests by scores of 2–1 and 4–2. In the second period of game four, the Oilers tied the score at 3–3 on a Craig Simpson goal. A few seconds later, the lights went out, plunging the Arena into darkness. The Oilers followed police with flashlights back to their locker room where they also showered and dressed by flashlight. An old four-thousand-watt transformer had failed, causing the blackout. The official league decision was to disregard the tie game as if it had never occurred, and move the series to Edmonton.

The Oilers took the replayed game in Edmonton and were leading game four by a score of 3–2, when Gretzky fed Craig Simpson a pass that Simpson converted into the Oilers' fourth goal. Edmonton sailed to an easy 6–3 victory, winning the Stanley Cup in what was considered (discounting the blacked-out contest) a four-game sweep. By winning their fourth Stanley Cup in five years, the Oilers had proven their dynasty status beyond any

*Wayne Gretzky looks for a pass as he skates in front of the Toronto net.*

question. The average age of the players on the Oilers' team was just twenty-five. It appeared to be a dynasty that would go on forever, but there was a great change brewing in Edmonton.

The Oilers' fourth Stanley Cup was a special triumph for Gretzky. He was voted MVP of the finals and his 10 assists and 13 points set a new record. Then, back in the locker room following the Cup-clinching game, Gretzky's teammates let him in on a secret; the Oilers had placed him on the trading block. For months Gretzky's family and teammates had heard that Edmonton's owner, Peter Pocklington, was seeking to trade Gretzky, but they had kept the rumor a secret for fear it would affect Gretzky's playoff performance.

Wayne Gretzky and actress Janet Jones were married on July 16, 1988, in what was billed as the Royal Wedding of Canada. There were over seven hundred guests invited. Hundreds of members of the media and a crowd of some ten thousand people also gathered outside the church, hoping to catch a glimpse of the couple. Few, if any, of the people in that crowd realized that the man they called a "national treasure" was about to be sold to a team in another country.[2]

The trade was announced at a press conference in Edmonton on August 8, 1988, with two hundred members of the media present. The Los Angeles Kings had paid a king's ransom for The Great One. Fifteen million dollars, three first-round draft picks, Jimmy Carson, and Martin Gelina were sent to Edmonton in exchange for Gretzky, his pal Marty McSorley, and Mike Krushelnyski. Wayne Gretzky sat on the podium wiping away tears as he said goodbye to the people of Edmonton. A year later, Gretzky looked back on that emotional day:

> At that point in time I felt like everyone else. I couldn't believe it was happening. It wasn't as if we had just lost. We had just won the Stanley Cup for the fourth time in five years. I had had arguably, my best playoffs ever. I won the Smythe, and all of a sudden I'm traded.[3]

In Edmonton and across the country, people were in a state of shock. The majority of the Canadian media characterized the trade as a "disgrace."

Gretzky was also leaving the Stanley Cup Champions for one of the least successful franchises in the NHL. In 1987–1988, Los Angeles finished eighteenth in the league. The Kings had never advanced to a Stanley Cup final in their twenty-two years of existence. Could Gretzky turn around the fortunes of the Los Angeles Kings?

# Chapter 6

# King of the Kings

In addition to his playing ability, another reason for Gretzky's enormous popularity is his patience and polite manner with people—particularly young people. Gretzky is never too busy to sign autographs for young fans, and he regularly participates in youth hockey camps during the off-season. One day, shortly after Wayne Gretzky and his wife arrived in Los Angeles, Gretzky was driving through Beverly Hills, following his wife's car. Suddenly, she stopped when she saw a group of young people playing roller hockey in the street. Mrs. Gretzky rolled down her window and shouted to them, "Hey guys, look who's in the car behind me." When they recognized The Great One, they rushed over for autographs. After signing for everyone, Gretzky drove away, amazed to find young people playing roller hockey in Beverly Hills.[1]

The Los Angeles Kings had come to be something of a laughing matter. Los Angeles, it was said, was a place where old hockey players came to die, a city that was basically indifferent toward professional hockey. Could Wayne Gretzky transform Los Angeles into a hockey town?[2]

This question did not take long to answer. Season ticket sales, which had been just four thousand, almost tripled; and for the first time in their history, the Kings sold out their home opener. With Magic Johnson sending over balloons, Roy Orbinson singing the national anthem, and a cluster of celebrities including Goldie Hawn, Michael J. Fox, and John Candy among the crowd of sixteen thousand, it certainly looked as if hockey had caught on in Hollywood.

Prior to the game against the Red Wings, the crowd responded with steady applause as each of the Kings was introduced at center ice. Then, as Gretzky emerged on the ice in his familiar number 99, the cheers turned into a sustained roar. Los Angeles was down 1–0 in the first period when Gretzky took his first shot as a King. The Kings had a two-man advantage as Dave Taylor sent a pass streaking to Gretzky at the goal. Gretzky raised his stick and fired a shot, beating Detroit's Greg Stefan. The goal tied the score and launched a new era for Los Angeles hockey: The Gretzky Age. Gretzky added three assists to his goal, as Los Angeles blew out Detroit, 8–2.

Gretzky's Los Angeles debut had been a complete success, both personally and for the Kings. Now he had another emotional game coming up on October 19. He would make his first appearance in Edmonton since the trade. Gretzky was gone but not forgotten in Edmonton. This had been proven back in August, just after the trade, when a six-foot-high bronze statue of Gretzky holding up the Stanley Cup was unveiled outside the Edmonton Coliseum.

Gretzky felt that the statue should not be erected until after he retired, but Edmontonians felt differently. Management for the Oilers did not participate in the ceremony, but Mark Messier, Kevin Lowe, David Semenko, and other team members did—in front of a full house of Oiler fans. Now the Edmonton Coliseum had another sellout crowd to welcome back The Great One. When Gretzky was announced before the game, he received a four minute standing ovation from Oilers' fans. For Gretzky, it was a mediocre game, as he managed just 2 assists in the Kings' 8–5 loss. But he would never forget the warm reception he received from the fans. For Gretzky, there would also be other moments of great triumph in Edmonton.

With Gretzky wearing their uniform, the Kings were a box-office success. There were questions, however. "Would The Great One's presence make a difference in the play of this team?" The answer was again yes. Many of Gretzky's teammates, aided by his playmaking skills and inspired by his presence, went on to have great seasons.

By the All-Star break, the Kings' record stood at 25–15–1, by far their best start in years. The All-Star Game was played in Edmonton, and Gretzky put on an all-star performance. With 1 goal and 2 assists, he was voted the game's MVP. Edmontonians would have another sad reminder of what The Great One could do during the playoffs.

Los Angeles finished the season at 42–31–7, nailing down second place in the Smythe Division and rising from eighteenth to fourth in the league. The Kings won twelve more games and acquired twenty-three more points than they had the previous season. In recognition of his contribution to the Kings' success, Gretzky was awarded his ninth Hart trophy as the NHL's Most Valuable Player.

As fate would have it, the Kings drew the Oilers

*Besides being an NHL star, Gretzky will often represent his native country in such international tournaments as The Canada Cup or the World Championships.*

in the first round of the playoffs. It was a hard-fought series, with the Kings battling back from a three games to one deficit to tie the Oilers after six games. The final game was played in Los Angeles. Gretzky scored the first goal in another hard-fought contest. With the score tied at 3–3, Gretzky sent a perfect pass to Bernie Nichols, who converted it into the goal that put the Kings up for good. In the final minutes, Gretzky shot another goal into an open net to seal the game at 6–3, and win the series for Los Angeles. Gretzky had quickly come back to haunt the Oilers, but the tough series had taken its toll on the Kings, who were then swept by Calgary in the second round of the playoffs.

Heading into the 1989–1990 season, Gretzky held over fifty NHL records. Now he stood poised to shatter another of his idol Gordie Howe's records. With the new season set to begin, he was just six points shy of Howe's all-time point record, 1,850. Heading into the sixth game of the season, he was just one point shy of Howe's record. Again, his fate was tied in to the Oilers as the Kings' next game was in Edmonton.

Gretzky's parents and wife, joined by Gordie Howe and NHL president John Ziegler, were on hand for the game. Just 4:32 into the contest, Gretzky tied the record with his 1,850 point—an assist on a Bernie Nichols goal. The Oilers rebounded with two goals before the Kings' Steve Duchesne tied the score at 2. Before the end of the first period, Gretzky had two opportunities to break the record, but Oilers' goalie Bill Ranford turned him back with two nice saves. In the second period, Gretzky took a pair of hard blows to the head. One hit, a high stick to the face, forced Gretzky to leave the game. With the score tied, 3–3, in the third period, Kevin Lowe put the Oilers ahead, 4–3, with a slap shot from the blue line. With the Kings down by a goal, Gretzky insisted on playing, but the score remained in favor of Edmonton through the first nineteen minutes of the final period. With the Kings desperate to tie the score with only a minute left to play, they pulled their goalie out of the net and attacked with a 6–5 advantage. Gretzky was hanging behind the net when Dave Taylor passed the puck from the far right corner to the front of the goal. Like a rocket, Gretzky shot out from behind the goal and back-handed the puck between Ranford and the post for a goal. In classic Gretzky style, The Great One had tied the game with just fifty-three seconds left on the clock—and also broke the all-time point record. The Edmonton Coliseum exploded, as Oiler fans gave their departed hero a three-minute standing ova-tion.[3] The game was stopped for ten minutes as

*Wayne Gretzky shares a candid moment with his daughter Paulina. Gretzky always makes sure that his family members are on hand to share in his personal accomplishments.*

Gretzky's father, his wife, Gordie Howe, Mark Messier, and league president Ziegler joined him at center ice for a ceremony marking the event.

Mark Messier presented Gretzky with a diamond bracelet that spelled out "1851." Gordie Howe told the crowd, "In all honesty, I've been looking forward to today. It's really nice for me to be a part of this." When Gretzky stepped to the microphone, he thanked his wife, his family, his teammates, and Gordie Howe: "Gordie is still the greatest in my mind and everyone else's mind," he said. The arena again erupted in cheers when Gretzky acknowledged that he scored 1,669 of his points as an Oiler. "An award like this takes a lot of teamwork. Both teams that are here today are definitely part of the record."[4]

Gretzky's great evening was not over. The game ended after regulation time in a 4–4 tie, and was sent into overtime. At 3:34 into overtime, Gretzky took a pass from Larry Robinson and scored the game-winning goal. Later, Peter Pocklington, the man who had traded Gretzky to Los Angeles, told a reporter, "There is no question that Wayne is the greatest player who ever played the game or ever will play the game." But Gretzky was not there to hear this. He was sitting with his family, Gordie Howe, and other friends, enjoying the glory of the moment.[5]

**FACT**

On October 15, 1989, Wayne Gretzky broke Gordie Howe's all-time point record by scoring his 1,851 point. It came on a goal against Edmonton. During the game, Gretzky used fourteen hockey sticks.

Gretzky and his family were enjoying life in Southern California, where Gretzky's interests were branching out beyond hockey. He was now co-owner with Bruce McNall of a race horse named Golden Pheasant. One of the reasons that Gretzky liked life in Los Angeles was because of the anonymity it provided him. Gretzky was now one of the most famous athletes in the world. In Edmonton, it seemed as if every time he went to a movie or stopped at a coffee shop, he made the newspapers. Los Angeles, because of its size and the presence of so many other celebrities, provided him with more peace, quiet, and privacy than he had in Edmonton.

As a hockey player, however, Gretzky felt there was a major disadvantage to a big city like Los Angeles. In smaller Edmonton, all of the players lived within twenty minutes of each other. This made socializing easier and helped keep the Oilers a close-knit team. In sprawling Los Angeles, where many of the players lived over an hour from each other, gathering off the ice was much less frequent. The Kings were just not that close.

There was a big difference in attitude between the Oilers and the Kings. The Oilers under hard-driving coach Glen Sather, were devoted to winning. The Kings under coach Robbie Ftorek were nowhere near as driven to win. From experience,

Gretzky knew that a team needed, beyond talent, a great camaraderie and a great will to win in order to make it earn a Stanley Cup. At this point in his career, there were two things that Gretzky wanted more than anything else—to break the all-time goal scoring record and to win another Stanley Cup.

For most of the season, the Kings remained in fourth place within their division. Gretzky missed several games in March due to a groin injury. Then on March 17, a back check from Alan Kerr caused him to miss the last eight games of the season. The Kings lost six of those eight contests. Despite the missed time, Gretzky again led the NHL with 142 points, but he failed to win his tenth Hart trophy as league MVP, as the Kings just managed to squeeze into the playoffs.

Los Angeles was not expected to do well against the Cup-defending Calgary Flames, its first-round opponents. But with Gretzky back in action, the Kings gave the hockey world a surprise. In the first game, played in Calgary, the Kings were down 3–1 in the third period, but fought back to win, 5–3. It was the greatest comeback in team history. The Kings battled the Flames to a 3–3 series tie and won the deciding seventh game in overtime. It was the second-straight year that the Gretzky-led Kings eliminated the defending Stanley Cup Champion in

**FACT**

On March 22, 1991, Wayne Gretzky and Bruce McNall purchased a rare Honus Wagner baseball trading card at Sothebys auction house for $451,000. This was the record price for a single item of sports memorabilia. The card has since been resold for $640,000 which remains the highest price ever paid for a single piece of sports memorabilia.

the first round of post-season play. As in the previous year, the tough series took its toll. With nine players hurt, including Gretzky, Los Angeles was swept by Edmonton in four-straight games. It had not been a good year for Los Angeles, but Gretzky was convinced that owner McNall and new coach Barry Melrose were as determined as he was to make the Kings a contender in the race for the Stanley Cup.

# Chapter 7

# Injury and Comeback

In July 1990, Wayne Gretzky and his wife celebrated the birth of their second child, a boy named Ty Robert Gretzky. Like his father, Ty would be on ice skates by the time he was two years old. With Wayne Gretzky approaching his thirtieth birthday, speculation also began about how much longer he would be able to sustain the level of playing excellence he had introduced to the NHL some eleven years earlier. As the Kings' management worked at building a contending team around him, Gretzky, however, continued to plow through NHL records.

On October 26, 1990, in the first period of a game against Winnipeg, Gretzky passed the puck to Tony Granato, who fed Tomas Sandstrom for a goal.

*Wayne Gretzky's father had put him in skates at a very young age, and Gretzky did the same with his son Ty. Only time will tell if Ty becomes a hockey star as well. Young Wayne Gretzky is shown here.*

Gretzky's assist gave him 2,000 points for his career. Following the game, Gretzky looked back on his first NHL point, scored back in the 1979–1980 season. Reporters asked Gretzky if he thought 3,000 points were obtainable before he retired. "When I got my 1,000th point I told people that 1,500 was reachable but that 2,000 was out of the question," Gretzky replied. "Now I say 2,500, but 3,000 is out of the question."[1] Some people felt that never again would a hockey player score two thousand points; but they were not so sure that Gretzky would not reach the three thousand plateau.

Gretzky acquired point 2,000 with 1,316 assists and 684 goals. Only three players in the history of the NHL had scored seven hundred or more goals: Gordie Howe (801), Marcel Dionne (717), and Phil Esposito (717); all three were retired. On January 3, 1991, Gretzky joined this exclusive club in grand style, with a hat trick against the New York Islanders. Then, on January 26, his thirtieth birthday, Gretzky had an answer for those who thought he might be slowing down. His answer was another hat trick and two assists for a five-point game in a 5–4 win over Vancouver. He netted his first goal of the evening just twelve seconds into the second period. In scoring his third goal, Gretzky displayed the artistry that made him the greatest player in the

**FACT**

On November 26, 1991, Wayne Gretzky, part owner of the Toronto Argonauts, was on hand in Winnipeg, Manitoba, Canada, watching his team defeat the Calgary Stampeders in the Grey Cup—the championship of Canadian football. Meanwhile, on the same day in Tokyo, Japan, Golden Pheasant, a horse co-owned by Gretzky, was winning the $2.7 million Japan Cup race.

game. After taking a feed from Tomas Sandstrom on the breakaway, Gretzky faked a shot to draw Canucks' goalie Kirk McLean out of the net. Then, he quickly circled behind the goal and flipped the puck into the empty net. In the closing moments of the game, Gretzky could have had a fourth goal, but he momentarily hesitated to shoot at an empty net and had the puck slapped away.

Some people were beginning to question whether Gretzky would ever lead the Kings into the Stanley Cup finals. Others accused him of being a prima donna who did not take his share of hits, lurking instead at the red line or behind the net until scoring opportunities appeared. Both complaints would vanish, the second following an injury that made it look as if The Great One's hockey days were over.

It started on April 28, 1992, following a game in which the Oilers knocked the Kings out of the playoffs. Gretzky's agent, Mike Barnett, came into the locker room to find Gretzky in street clothes, pale, and bathed in sweat. A team doctor diagnosed the problem as a "rib injury."[2] Several days later, Barnett and Gretzky were having breakfast when Gretzky was hit with a bolt of pain. He had to stretch out in the restaurant booth in order to relieve the symptoms. The pain subsided, and several days later the Gretzky family went on a planned vacation to Hawaii. There, the pain flared up again, forcing Gretzky to check into a local hospital. Back in Los Angeles, the condition subsided to the point where he was able to implement his usual rigorous off-season traning program.

Gretzky reported to the 1992 training camp in the best condition of his career. "He went into camp feeling like lightning," his wife said. "We just had our third child then . . ."[3] Then Gretzky awoke one night in searing pain. What was thought in April to be a "rib injury" returned worse than ever. Several days of testing determined that Gretzky, in fact, had a herniated thoracic disc in his spinal column. The injury usually occurred in the lower back, where the spine is widest and most likely to heal. Mario Lemieux once had a lower-back herniation and successfully returned to play hockey. Gretzky's herniation, however, was at the point where the spinal column was at its narrowest. A specialist pronounced it a one-in-a-million injury. The injury had resulted from the countless blind-side hits and back checks Gretzky had endured during twenty-five years of playing organized hockey.

Doctors pointed out that surgery could lead to complications that might result in paralysis. Opting against surgery, Gretzky went home to rest and consider his future. It did not take much inactivity for Gretzky to realize what he had to do. He soon became a regular fixture in the Kings' training room. "I remember coming in here and seeing him work out two, three hours a day," said the Kings' Luc Robitaille, "I think he realized when he was hurt how much he loved to play the game."[4]

On January 6, less than four months after his spinal injury was diagnosed, Gretzky returned to the ice. The fans were handed "Welcome Back Wayne" placards as they entered the Forum, and shouts of "Let's go Wayne!" continued through the national anthem. Gretzky's presence made little difference that night, however, as the Kings lost to Tampa Bay, 6–3. As the season progressed, it became clear that Gretzky was rusty after his thirty-nine-game layoff. He played sixteen games, from January 10 to February 15 without scoring a single goal. It was the longest drought of his career. People began to wonder not when, but if they would ever see the old Gretzky again. Even Gretzky himself began to get discouraged; several times he considered quitting.

Then suddenly on February 15, against Minnesota, Gretzky exploded for 1 goal and 4 assists in a 10–5 rout of the North Stars. From this point on, his game continued to improve over the remainder of the season. It had been a long struggle, but the old Gretzky was back.

One benefit that resulted from Gretzky's absence and slow return to his usual game form was the fact that his teammates had to rely more on themselves—and not The Great One—to run the show. As a result, they began to come together as a team, better than they ever had before. Gretzky worked his way into mid-season form just in time for the playoffs. The Kings were in good shape as they headed into post-season play.

The experts felt that, with or without Gretzky, the Kings were not likely to advance very far in the playoffs. When Los Angeles powered its way past Vancouver in the first round, it was considered an upset. When the Kings defeated Calgary behind relentlessly brilliant play by Gretzky, it was considered an even bigger upset. But Gretzky or no Gretzky, the experts said, there was no way the Kings would get past the powerful Toronto Maple Leafs in the Campbell Conference finals. It began to look as if they were right, as Gretzky started to struggle. The Kings found themselves down three games to two, one loss away from elimination.

Gretzky responded by scoring the winning goal in overtime of game six, forcing the series back to Toronto for the seventh and deciding contest. With 3 goals and 1 assist, Gretzky almost singlehandedly propelled the Kings past the Maple Leafs 5–4—and into the Stanley Cup Finals for the first time in their twenty-six-year history. Over that period, the Kings had gone through seventeen coaches, five general managers, three owners, and countless players before finding the key to the finals—the trade that brought Wayne Gretzky to Los Angeles. How did Gretzky feel about it? "I've played fourteen years," he said. "I don't think I've ever got more satisfaction than I did winning this series."[5]

The Kings found themselves facing the Montreal Canadiens in the finals. Winners of twenty-three Stanley Cups, the Canadiens were the most successful franchise in NHL history, and very powerful on their home ice. The Canadiens were defending an eight-game winning streak at home as the finals began at their rink, the Montreal Forum. It was another playoff game decided by the "Gretzky Factor." Gretzky figured in all five goals in the Kings' 4–1 win before a stunned sellout crowd of nearly eighteen thousand people. Gretzky scored 2 goals in the game—one for each team. While back checking on defense late in the first period, he desperately lunged to clear the puck through the crease; instead, the puck went past Los Angeles goalie Kelly Hrudey and into the net for a Montreal goal. All

*After returning from a severe back injury, Gretzky guided the Kings into the 1993 Stanley Cup Finals.*

Gretzky could do was skate away, slowly shaking his head. With the score tied at 1–1 in the second period, Gretzky came back to score another goal (this time for the Kings), at a near-impossible angle. He also added 3 assists in the Kings' surprise victory. "Gretzky toyed with us tonight," said Montreal coach Jacques Demers, following the game, "this was The Great One we saw tonight."[6]

If the Montreal fans were stunned by game one, they were in a state of shock in game two. With less than two minutes left in the game, Los Angeles held a 2–1 lead. Then with little to lose, Montreal coach Demers asked the officials to measure Marty McSorley's stick. It was found that the stick exceeded the legal curvature by a quarter of an inch. McSorley was sent off to the penalty box, and Montreal, with a one-man advantage, was able to score on their power play to tie the game with 1:13 left on the clock. Montreal went on to win in overtime. The defeat broke Los Angeles' back. Although they fought valiantly through the rest of the finals (losing the next two games in overtime as well), Montreal won the series and the Stanley Cup in five games.[7]

Gretzky had been riding an emotional roller coaster all season. First there was the shock and the fear following his spinal cord injury. Then came the long, hard rehabilitation period, as he worked to bring his game back to its former excellence. Finally, there was the struggle and joy of leading the Kings into the finals—only to lose to Montreal.

Gretzky was just thirty-two years old, and still at the top of his game, but he was exhausted. In the press conference following the finals, a reporter asked, "Wayne, after taking the Kings this far, are you hungry to come back next year?" Gretzky hesitated for a moment and said, "I'm not sure." The room fell silent. When pressed by reporters, Gretzky elaborated, "I'm going to sit back over the next few days, talk to my wife, and decide what my future is."[8]

# Chapter 8

# The Greatest One

In late June 1993, at the youth hockey camp he ran outside of Quebec City, Gretzky expressed concern about this future in hockey, "I don't want to embarrass myself," he said.[1] Despite his concerns, however, there was no way Gretzky could quit hockey. Kings' owner McNall, however, did not share Gretzky's worries about his future playing ability. Gretzky signed a three-year, $25.5 million contract with the Kings. The size of the contract sparked a controversy in the press. At the time, the contract was the largest given any professional athlete. Some argued that it was simply too much money, but most writers came down on Gretzky's side of the issue. Gretzky's supporters argued that aside from his achievements, he was the perfect ambassador for hockey.

As the new season began, Gretzky picked up where he had left off prior to his spinal injury, leading the NHL in scoring. Back to his old self, Gretzky set his sights on one of the last major hockey records that he did not already hold—Gordie Howe's all-time NHL goal record of 801. Heading into the season, Gretzky stood just thirty-seven goals shy of Howe's record. Would The Great One break the record this season?

The question was answered in late March 1994. On March 20 in San Jose, Gretzky tied the record by scoring two goals against the Sharks in a 6–6 tie. Now the March 23 game at the Los Angeles Forum against the Canucks was the hottest ticket in town, as Gretzky stood poised to shatter the record. Present among the sellout crowd at the Forum was the Gretzky family—his wife; their three children, Paulina, Ty, and Trevor; his mother; and perhaps most important to Gretzky, his father. Two years earlier, Walter Gretzky has suffered a brain aneurism, a potentially life-threatening blood clot. It was Walter Gretzky who had put Wayne on skates when he was two years old, and who guided him into organized hockey when he was just six years old. When Wayne lost three teeth in a hockey game at age twelve, it was Walter Gretzky who made him laugh by saying, "Well, at least you look like a hockey player now."[2]

Walter Gretzky had always been there to guide and counsel his son on the path to hockey immortality. So nothing was more important to Wayne Gretzky than the fact that his father was almost fully recovered from his illness, and there to see him add a crowning achievement to his great career.

It was also fitting that the Kings' Marty McSorley, Gretzky's old teammate on the Oilers and longtime close friend, fed him the pass with which he broke the record. With fourteen minutes gone in the second period, and with the Kings on a power play, Luc Robitaille brought the puck into the Vancouver zone and passed off to Gretzky. As they had done so many times before, Gretzky passed to McSorley, and streaked down to the left circle as McSorley skated at full speed down the right side. Vancouver goalie Kirk McLean came out of the goal to cut off McSorley's angle, and the trap was set. McSorley raised his stick as if to shoot, but instead passed the puck across the crease to Gretzky who fired it into the empty net. It was done; with goal 802, Wayne Gretzky was now the greatest scorer in NHL history. As the Forum exploded in cheers, Gretzky was seen raising his arms, turning towards his family, and mouthing the words, "I did it, I did it!"[3] He was swamped by his teammates, as the Forum fans continued to thunder out their approval. The first thing

**FACT**

Because he missed thirty-nine games due to injury at the start of the 1993–1994 season, Wayne Gretzky was not selected to the All-Star team for the first time in his career. He then became the first player in NHL history to be appointed to the team by the president of the league.

Gretzky did was to skate over to the celebrity box and whisper something into his father's ear. The game was then halted for a ceremony at mid-ice. NHL Commissioner Gary Bettman presented Gretzky with a score sheet of every game in which he had scored a goal. Bettman then said, "You've always been The Great One, but tonight you became the greatest."[4]

Gretzky finished the season with 130 points (38 goals and 92 assists), winning his tenth scoring title in fourteen years. But the Kings failed to make it to the finals, as they would again in 1994–1995 post-season play.

By the start of the 1995–1996 season, the Kings were a team in transition. Gretzky was a veteran on a team undergoing an extensive rebuilding program. He desperately wanted to win another Stanley Cup, however.

In January 1996, with the Kings rated twentieth of twenty-six teams, Gretzky made it known that he wanted to be traded. Despite his large salary, a number of teams were interested in acquiring The Great One, particularly the New York Rangers and the St. Louis Blues. The Rangers entered into lengthy negotiations with the Kings and Gretzky's agent, Mike Barnett. But the negotiations fell through, at least for the time being. At this point, St. Louis made its bid for Gretzky.

On February 27, 1996, the Kings' management called a press conference to announce that Gretzky had been traded to the Blues for Roman Vopat, Patrice Tardif, Craig Johnson, and a first round draft choice. The Blues certainly needed him. With the season sixty-two games old, St. Louis was struggling to make it into the playoffs.

Gretzky joined his new team on the road in Vancouver, where he scored a goal in a 2–2 tie. It was to be a scary, bumpy start with the Blues—the bump being to Gretzky's head. In his second game for St. Louis, in Edmonton, Gretzky was elbowed on the side of the head by Oiler Kelly Buchberger. The blow knocked him flat on the ice, unconscious. Gretzky lay motionless for several minutes as the sellout crowd fell silent. Eventually, he was revived and helped off the ice by several of his teammates. A fight ensued between the Blues' Murray Baron and Buchberger, after which St. Louis went on to win the game, 4–3.[5] Gretzky suffered a minor concussion, but he pronounced himself "ninety-nine percent" for his at-home debut on March 5. Before the game against the Florida Panthers, The Great One received a long standing ovation from Blues' fans when he was introduced last as the new team

*Toward the end of the 1995–96 season, Gretzky was traded to the St. Louis Blues where he would attempt to lead the struggling team to a playoff spot.*

captain. Gretzky did not score in the 2–0 win over the Panthers, but in his next game he had 2 assists in a 4–2 loss against Calgary.

As has been the case in Los Angeles, Gretzky's arrival in town was a box-office bonanza for the Blues. The huge, new Keil Center, seating over twenty thousand people, was sold out for the rest of the season.[6]

Gretzky finished the season with 23 goals and 79 assists for 102 points. This marked the fifteenth season in which he had scored one hundred or more points, extending his own NHL record. With Gretzky's trademark creative playmaking, the Blues managed to make it into the playoffs.

Gretzky led the playoffs in scoring after the Blues defeated Toronto in the first round of post-season play. Now they faced a formidable challenge in the Detroit Red Wings, who had won a record-setting 62 games during the regular season. They had also finished the season fifty-one points ahead of the Blues. Further, St. Louis first-string goalie, Grant Fuhr, was lost to injury during the Toronto series. Many people expected that St. Louis would be swept by Detroit.

It appeared at first as if the series would be a Detroit rout, as the Red Wings took the first two games. Then Gretzky kicked in. In five of the seven playoff contests, games were decided by one point. St. Louis bounced back by winning the third game; and the Blues evened the series at two games each by taking the fourth contest, 1–0. The lone goal was courtesy of Wayne Gretzky. Playing as if he were ageless, Gretzky led the Blues to three-straight wins, forcing a seventh contest at the Joe Louis Arena in Detroit.

The seventh game was a classic, the crowning contest to a thrilling series. It was estimated that Gretzky had a grueling forty minutes of playing time in a game that went scoreless for eighty-one minutes, and went on for over four hours. Finally, in the second overtime period, Detroit's captain, Steve Yzerman, fired a slap shot from just inside the St. Louis blue line to beat Blues' goalie, Jon Casey, and win the game 1–0.[7] Although the Blues were eliminated, their performance in this series put a positive ending on what would otherwise have been a dismal season for St. Louis. Everyone agreed that St. Louis's credible post-season showing would have been impossible without Gretzky.

In the off-season, Gretzky faced a major decision. On July 1, 1996, he was scheduled to become an unrestricted free agent for the first time in his career. This meant that if he did not re-sign with St. Louis, he was free to sign with any other team in the NHL. The Blues reportedly offered Gretzky a contract worth

$14 million for two years. There were, however, another six or seven teams, including the New York Rangers, interested in acquiring his services.

Money was not the prime motivation for Gretzky as he considered his options. He was presented with the opportunity to be reunited with his close friend Mark Messier, then captain of the New York Rangers. Besides Messier, the Ranger roster was clustered with other old friends of Gretzky's from the Oilers' glory years, such as Marty McSorley, Jeff Beukeboom, and Jari Kurri. Gretzky took a considerable pay cut for the chance to try to earn another Stanley Cup with his former teammates. On July 21, 1996, at a press conference in Madison Square Garden in New York, it was announced that Gretzky had signed a two-year contract with the Rangers for a reported $10 million dollars.[8]

Not all New York Rangers' fans were happy to see Gretzky join the team. Some pointed out that Gretzky, who would be thirty-six years old on January 26, was limited to 45 games during the 1992–1993 season and 48 games in the 1994–1995 campaign due to injuries. Some people wondered whether it was a good idea to pay a player his age— even The Great One—that kind of money. After all, his durability could only be a question mark. Some suggested that maybe it would be a better idea to spend the money on younger players.

Gretzky answered the critics by playing in all 82 Rangers' regular season games in 1996–1997 and by leading the team with 97 total points (25 goals and 78 assists). This was good enough for fourth best in the NHL. Gretzky's brilliant passing ability not only dazzled the fans and won games, but aided in the development of the Rangers' young players like the Niklas Sundstrom who scored just 9 goals in

*Wayne Gretzky and Mark Messier seem to be enjoying themselves during the 1984 Canada Cup. These two good friends were reunited when Gretzky signed with the New York Rangers prior to the 1996–97 season.*

1995–1996. Playing at right wing with Gretzky, Sundstrom raised his goal total to 24 for the 1996–1997 campaign. Still, with injuries to captain Mark Messier and others, the Rangers finished with a disappointing 38-34-10 record, just making it into the playoffs.

The Rangers drew the Florida Panthers as their first opponent in postseason play. Most experts felt that New York would not advance beyond the first round. Gretzky looked at the situation differently. He had the ninth playoff hat trick of his career, and his usual great play-making, lead the Rangers right past the Panthers. But the Rangers next would meet the Eastern Conference Champion New Jersey Devils. Hardly anyone believed the Rangers would get by the powerhouse Devils—except perhaps Gretzky and his teammates. In the major upset of the playoffs, the Rangers eliminated the Devils in five games. Next, in the Stanley Cup semifinals against Philadelphia, Gretzky again astounded the hockey world with his tenth career postseason hat trick.

The Rangers fell to the Flyers in five games and Philadelphia went off to meet it's own brick wall in the form of the Detroit Red Wings who swept the series for the Stanley Cup Championship. However, everyone agreed on one thing. Father Time would have to wait—Wayne Gretzky remained The Great One.

Whether Gretzky and the rest of the Rangers manage to make it into the Stanley Cup finals remains to be seen. But one thing is for certain— Gretzky has earned a place among the greatest professional athletes who have ever lived. He has rewritten the hockey record book. His all-time goal record and his impact on hockey are frequently compared to Babe Ruth's home run records and Ruth's overall impact on the game of baseball. With his home run exploits in the 1920s, Ruth drew fans to baseball in unprecedented numbers. Through his great accomplishments and his skilled, nonviolent approach to hockey, Wayne Gretzky has played a key role in elevating the appeal of the game to its current, unquestioned status as a first-tier sport.

One more personal challenge lies ahead for Gretzky. Gretzky has already eclipsed 2500 points. Can he achieve the impossible and score 3000 points before he retires? Unfortunately, New York's success of 1997 did not carry over into 1998. While the Rangers struggled, Wayne Gretzky had yet another great season. His 90 points led the team, and was tied with Pavel Bure of Vancouver for third in the league. Gretzky was also tied for the league lead in assists, matching Jaromir Jagr's total of 67. Gretzky proved he still has plenty of hockey left in him.

# Chapter Notes

## Chapter 1

1. Lisa Dillman, "No. 99 Gets Goals No. 802—Now He's No. 1 on List," *The Los Angeles Times*, March 24, 1994, p. C1.

2. Ibid.

3. Jay Privman, "Great One Becomes NHL's Greatest," *The New York Times*, March 24, 1994, p. B13.

4. Joe LaPointe, "Rangers Graves Sets a Record of His Own," *The New York Times*, March 24, 1994, p. B13.

## Chapter 2

1. Walter Gretzky with Jim Taylor, *Gretzky, From Backyard Rink to Stanley Cup* (New York: Avon Books, 1984), pp. 38–43.

2. Ibid., p. 47.

3. Kevin Allen, "Even As Gretzky Nears Goal Mark, Howe Still His Hero," *USA Today*, February 3, 1994, p. C6.

4. Wayne Gretzky with Rick Reilly, *Gretzky: An Autobiography* (New York: HarperCollins, 1990), pp. 19–20.

5. Allen, p. C6.

6. Gretzky with Reilly, p. 20.

7. Ibid.

8. Ibid., pp. 32–33.

9. Ibid., pp. 114–118.

10. Ibid.

11. Ibid., pp. 32–33.

12. Ibid., pp. 35–36.

## Chapter 3

1. Lisa Dillman, "Gretzky Ready for Number 802," *The Los Angeles Times*, March 23, 1994, p. C1.

2. Garr Kvender, "Another Great One Showed Him Howe He Could Get Even," *Los Angeles Times*, October 16, 1989, p. C12.

3. Wayne Gretzky with Rick Reilly, *Gretzky: An Autobiography* (New York: HarperCollins, 1990), pp. 64, 66.

4. Ibid.

5. Kevin Dupont, "Oilers Win 5-2, to End Islanders' Cup Reign," *The New York Times*, March 20, 1984, sec. 5, pp. 1, 6.

6. Ibid.

## Chapter 4

1. Wayne Gretzky with Rick Reilly, *Gretzky: An Autobiography* (New York: HarperCollins, 1990), pp. 89–90.

2. Ibid., p. 101.

3. Ibid., p. 125.

4. Craig Wolff, "Oilers Perplexed by Loss of Opener," *The New York Times*, May 22, 1985, p. B13.

5. Gretzky with Reilly, p. 90.

6. Robin Finn, "Oilers Win in Overtime for 2-0 Margin," *The New York Times*, May 21, 1987, p. D23.

7. Robin Finn, "Oilers Take to Defense and Win Stanley Cup," *The New York Times*, June 1, 1987, pp. C1–2.

## Chapter 5

1. Wayne Gretzky with Rick Reilly, *Gretzky: An Autobiography* (New York: HarperCollins, 1990), p. 67.

2. Steve Wulf, "The Great Wedding," *Sports Illustrated*, July 25, 1988, pp. 9–12.

3. Tracy Dodds, "King For a Year," *The Los Angeles Times*, August 9, 1989, part 3, pp. 1, 10.

## Chapter 6

1. Mike Downey, "The King Arrives," *The Los Angeles Times*, May 31, 1993, pp. C1, C4.

2. Ibid.

3. Tracy Dodds, "Wayne Gretzky: 1852," *The Los Angeles Times*, October 16, 1989. p. C14.

4. Associated Press, "Gretzky Gets Record," *The New York Times*, October 16, 1989, p. C1.

5. Ibid.

## Chapter 7

1. Lisa Dillman, "Gretzky Nets 2000th," *The Los Angeles Times*, October 27, 1990, pp. C1, C8.

2. Jim Murray, "Grezky Back From Injury," *The Los Angeles Times*, June 5, 1993, p. T9.

3. Ibid.

4. Ibid.

5. Lisa Dillman, "Game 7 Victory is Great One," *The Los Angeles Times*, June 4, 1993, p. C1.

6. Lisa Dillman, "Kings Win at Follow the Leader," *The Los Angeles Times*, June 2, 1993, pp. C1, C7.

7. Lisa Dillman, "Kings Beaten by a Hat Trick," *The Los Angeles Times*, June 4, 1993, p. C1.

8. Mike Penner, "Gretzky Bombshell Is Felt by Both Teams," *Los Angeles Times*, June 10, 1993, p. C7.

## Chapter 8

1. Lisa Dillman, "Gretzky Doesn't Talk Like a Quitter," *The Los Angeles Times*, June 28, 1993, p. C2.

2. Wayne Gretzky with Rick Reilly, *Gretzky: An Autobiography* (New York: HarperCollins, 1990), p. 73.

3. Jay Privman, "Great One Becomes NHL's Greatest," *The New York Times*, February 4, 1996, p. C8.

4. Ibid.

5. Associated Press, "Gretzky Suffers Concussion in 2nd Game with Blues," *The New York Times*, February 4, 1996 p. C8.

6. Joe LaPointe, "Gretzky Has Brought Fans if Not Victories to Blues," *The New York Times*, April 1, 1996, p. C8.

7. Joe LaPointe, "Red Wings Advance in Overtime Thriller," *The New York Times*, May 17, 1996, p. B1.

8. Joe LaPointe, "Rangers Sign Gretzky to a Two-Year Contract," *The New York Times*, July 21, 1996, section 8, pp. 1, 10.

# Career Statistics

| Season | Team | League | GP | G | A | PTS | PIM |
|--------|------|--------|-----|-----|-------|-------|-----|
| 1979–80 | Edmonton | NHL | 79 | 51 | 86 | 137 | 21 |
| 1980–81 | Edmonton | NHL | 80 | 55 | 109 | 164 | 28 |
| 1981–82 | Edmonton | NHL | 80 | 92 | 120 | 212 | 26 |
| 1982–83 | Edmonton | NHL | 80 | 71 | 125 | 196 | 59 |
| 1983–84 | Edmonton | NHL | 74 | 87 | 118 | 205 | 39 |
| 1984–85 | Edmonton | NHL | 80 | 73 | 135 | 208 | 52 |
| 1985–86 | Edmonton | NHL | 80 | 52 | 163 | 215 | 46 |
| 1986–87 | Edmonton | NHL | 79 | 62 | 121 | 183 | 28 |
| 1987–88 | Edmonton | NHL | 64 | 40 | 109 | 149 | 24 |
| 1988–89 | Los Angeles | NHL | 78 | 54 | 114 | 168 | 26 |
| 1989–90 | Los Angeles | NHL | 73 | 40 | 102 | 142 | 42 |
| 1990–91 | Los Angeles | NHL | 78 | 41 | 122 | 163 | 16 |
| 1991–92 | Los Angeles | NHL | 74 | 31 | 90 | 121 | 34 |
| 1992–93 | Los Angeles | NHL | 45 | 16 | 49 | 65 | 6 |
| 1993–94 | Los Angeles | NHL | 81 | 38 | 92 | 130 | 20 |
| 1994–95 | Los Angeles | NHL | 48 | 11 | 37 | 48 | 6 |
| 1995–96 | Los Angeles/ St. Louis | NHL | 80 | 23 | 79 | 102 | 34 |
| 1996–97 | New York Rangers | NHL | 82 | 25 | 72 | 97 | 28 |
| 1997–98 | New York Rangers | NHL | 82 | 23 | 67 | 90 | 28 |
| **NHL Totals** | | | 1,417 | 885 | 1,910 | 2,795 | 563 |

**GP**=Games Played
**G**=Goals
**A**=Assists

**PTS**=Points
**PIM**=Penalty in Minutes

# Where to Write
# Wayne Gretzky

Mr. Wayne Gretzky
c/o New York Rangers
Madison Square Garden
New York, NY 10010

# Index

**A**

Anderson, Glenn, 32, 35, 38

**B**

Barnett, Mike, 76, 88–89
Beukeboom, Jeff, 93
Bossy, Mike, 48
Buchberger, Kelly, 89
Bumbacco, Angelo, 21

**C**

Carson, Jimmy, 60
Casey, John, 92
Ciccarelli, Dino, 24
Clark, Bobby, 44
Coffey, Paul, 32, 41, 47, 51

**D**

Demers, Jacques, 82
Dionne, Marcel, 31, 75
Duchesne, Steve, 67

**E**

Edmonton Oilers, 8, 11, 26, 27,
    30, 31, 32, 36–37, 39–40,
    46, 47, 48, 49, 52, 56, 57,
    63, 66, 67, 69, 70, 72, 76,
    87, 93
Esposito, Phil, 23, 35, 75

**F**

Fogolin, Lee, 38
Ftorek, Robbie, 70
Fuhr, Grant, 39, 46, 50, 91

**G**

Gelina, Martin, 60
Granato, Tony, 73
Graves, Adam, 11
Gretzky, Brent, 40
Gretzky, Mary, 14, 15
Gretzky, Paulina, 86
Gretzky, Phyllis, 11, 13, 20

Gretzky, Trevor, 86
Gretzky, Ty Robert, 73
Gretzky, Walter, 11, 13–14, 16, 19,
    20, 69, 86–87
Gretzky, Wayne
    breaks record for assists in
        a season, 36, 46, 49
    breaks record for career
        assists, 55
    breaks record for career
        goals, 9, 86
    breaks record for career
        points, 8, 67, 69
    breaks record for goals in a
        season, 36
    breaks record for points in
        a season, 36, 49
    childhood, 13–16, 18–21,
        23–24
    marries Janet Jones, 59
    scores 2000th point, 75
    signs with Indianapolis
        Racers, 25
    signs with New York
        Rangers, 93
    sold to Edmonton Oilers,
        26
    sustains severe back injury,
        77
    traded to Los Angeles
        Kings, 59–60
    traded to St. Louis Blues, 89

**H**

Hanlon, Glen, 30
Herbert, John, 18
Hextall, Ron, 51, 53
Hockey Night in Canada, 14, 15
Howe, Gordie, 8–9, 15, 18, 23, 24,
    29, 55, 66, 69, 75, 86
Hrudey, Kelly, 80
Hughes, Pat, 36

## I

Indianapolis Racers, 25, 27

## J

Johnson, Craig, 89
Jones, Janet, 11, 59, 69, 77, 86

## K

Kerr, Alan, 71
Krushelnyski, Mike, 60
Kurri, Jari, 32, 38, 40, 46, 47, 51, 56, 93

## L

Lafleur, Guy, 31
Lemieux, Mario, 56, 77
Lindstrom, Will, 47–48
Liut, Mike, 44
London Knights, 24
Los Angeles Kings, 7–9, 11, 34, 36–37, 47, 51, 55, 60, 62, 66, 69, 70, 71–72, 73, 76, 78, 79, 80, 82, 83, 85, 87, 88, 89
Lowe, Kevin, 30, 32, 41, 55, 63, 67
Lumley, Dave, 40

## M

Maholvich, Frank, 15
Martin, Dick, 16
McLean, Kirk, 76, 87
McNall, Bruce, 70, 71
McPherson, Muzz, 21
McSorley, Marty, 9, 60, 82, 87, 93
Melanson, Roland, 40
Melrose, Larry, 72
Messier, Mark, 30, 32, 41, 55, 63, 69, 93
Moog, Andy, 46
Murray, Tom, 47

## N

New York Islanders, 34, 36, 37, 38, 39–40, 75
New York Rangers, 11, 23, 88, 93

Nichols, Bernie, 66, 67

## O

Ottawa 67's, 23, 24

## P

Peeters, Pete, 35
Philadelphia Flyers, 31, 34–35, 46, 48, 49, 51, 55
Pocklington, Peter, 59, 69

## R

Ranford, Bill, 67
Richard, Maurice, 34
Robinson, Larry, 69
Robitaille, Luc, 9, 78, 87

## S

St. Louis Blues, 88, 91, 92, 93
Sandstrom, Tomas, 73, 76
San Jose Sharks, 96
Sather, Glen, 26, 27, 31, 34, 70
Semenko, Dave, 39, 63
Siegr, Jiri, 9
Simpson, Craig, 57
Smith, Billy, 38, 39, 40
Smith, Bobby, 24
Smith, Steve, 50, 53
Stefan, Greg, 63

## T

Tardif, Patrice, 89
Taylor, Dave, 62, 67

## V

Vernon, Mike, 56
Vopat, Roman, 89

## W

World Hockey Association (WHA), 24, 29, 30

## Y

Yzerman, Steve, 92

## Z

Ziegler, John, 66, 69